Bibliographic information published by the German National Library:

The German National Library lists this publication in the National Bibliography; detailed bibliographic data are available on the Internet at http://dnb.dnb.de .

Imprint:

Copyright © 2015 GRIN Verlag, Open Publishing GmbH
Print and binding: Books on Demand GmbH, Norderstedt Germany
ISBN: 9783668228597

This book at GRIN:

http://www.grin.com/en/e-book/321569/an-overview-of-the-national-research-output-and-the-situation-of-tunisian

Houcemeddine Turki, Manel Turki

An overview of the National Research output and the situation of Tunisian Universities

GRIN Publishing

An overview of the National Research output and situation of the Tunisian Universities

Houcemeddine Turki[a], Manel Turki[b]

[a] B.Sc. Student, Faculty of Medicine of Sfax, University of Sfax, Sfax, Tunisia
[b] Associate Professor, Faculty of Pharmacy, University of Monastir, Monastir, Tunisia

Abstract

Using the Ranking of Tunisian Scientists that was issued in 2014, we ranked Tunisian Universities in order to have an overview of the national research situation and standings and in order to explain their results in international classifications and ranking like ARWU and Leiden Ranking. The analysis confirmed the standings of Tunisian universities in several rankings like Leiden, ARWU and THE Rankings and proved that several classifications are not based on research performances of universities like 4icu and Webometrics. It explained the deficiency of the research performances of Tunisian universities by the lack of originality in the choice of research topics in some fields, by the lack of activity of several institutions and by the lack of initiatives of the administrations of the Universities to promote their research situation.

Keywords: Tunisian Universities, Research output, Efficient Productivity, International Classifications

Introduction

University Ranking has always been an important indicator of university excellence in Research (Van Raan, 2005; Liu, Cheng, & Liu, 2005; Docampo, 2010; Ioannidis, et al., 2007). That is why several general or specific rankings using different Bibliometric (Publication Analysis), Scientometric (Citation Analysis) and Altmetric (Analysis of Internet Statistics) metrics (Alaşehir, 2010; Liu, Cheng, & Liu, 2005; Van Raan, 2005; Aguillo, Ortega, & Fernández, 2008; Cheng & Liu, 2007). Many countries have interested in ameliorating their standings in these rankings to better their worldwide research reputation by writing papers about the issue and by developing methods to promote their standings (Harfi & Mathieu, 2006; Aghion, Dewatripont, Hoxby, Sapir, & Mas-Colell, 2007). However and although the topic seems to interest and influence politicians in developing countries (Salmi & Saroyan, 2007; Hazelkorn, 2007) mainly thanks to the amelioration of expenditure of Tunisian government in promoting public Higher education (Naim & Rahman, 2008), limited papers and works are done about the subject in Tunisia and even the standings of Tunisian Universities differ from one region to another ranging from 600 (in URAP and Leiden) to 4000 (in 4icu) for the best Tunisian university. Even the leading Tunisian university differs from one ranking to another. In fact, the University of Sfax leads Leiden and URAP rankings, the University of Sousse leads 4icu and Webometrics Ranking, the University of Monastir leads OIC ranking, the University of Tunis Manar leads ARWU, THE, JC and SIR Rankings...

In this research paper, we will give a clear and concise overview about the National Research output and situation of the Tunisian Universities.

List of the main International Rankings:

Name	Full Name
ARWU	Academic Ranking of World Universities
URAP	University Ranking of Academic Performance
THE	Times Higher Education Ranking
Webometrics	Webometrics Ranking
4icu	4icu Ranking
OIC (SESRTCIC, 2007)	Organization of Islamic Conference Ranking
SIR	Scopus Institutional Ranking
Leiden	Leiden Ranking
JC	Africa Journals Consortium Ranking

Methods

It is clear and evident that scientists with best h-indexes in a given country are full professors and Heads of research departments. These scientists are monitoring scientific research in their institutions because they are supervising and involved in the works of Ph.D. and M.Sc. students of their faculties (Mangematin & Robin, 2003) and because they are leading international collaboration structures and by that involved in the highly cited papers of their institution made through international collaboration (Wagner & Leydesdorff, 2005). Consequently, the standings of these professors in national h-index ranking can give an overview about the publication and citation nationwide standings of a given university. That is why we will use the reported affiliations in the ranking of Tunisian scientists we have made in 2014 (Turki & Turki, 2014) to rank Tunisian universities and explain their research situation and their standings in the international rankings. Scientists will be divided into five categories according to their disciplines using Pierce's principle (Turki & Turki, 2014): *Mathematics, Engineering and Computer Science, Medical Sciences and Pharmacology, Chemistry and Materials Science, Physics, Social Sciences and Humanities* and *Biology and Geological Sciences*. The overall number of the ranked scientists for each university as well as the number of scientists for each category and university are calculated and then analyzed. As Google Scholar five year h-index / Google Scholar h-index = 0.8 (Turki & Turki, 2014), the ranking will give an overview about the historical nationwide research standings of Tunisian universities as well as the current standings of Tunisian universities.

Results and Discussion

1. Université de Tunis Manar and Université de Sfax

As shown in Table 1, it is clear clearly that the Université de Tunis Manar is the first ranked university and the Université de Sfax is the second ranked university confirming the result of most of the research rankings.

Field	Université de Tunis Manar		Université de Sfax	
	Scientists	Rank	Scientists	Rank
Mathematics, Engineering and Computer Science	5	1	2	4
Medical Sciences and Pharmacology	35	1	20	3
Chemistry and Materials Science	5	1	2	2
Physics	2	3	1	4
Social Sciences and Humanities	0	1	0	1
Biology and Geological Sciences	5	3	26	1
Overall	52	1	51	2

Fig. 1: Dispersion of Scientists of Université de Tunis Manar and Université de Sfax according to their disciplines

This seems to be evident as the University of Tunis Manar has the greatest number of professors (2975 professors in 2012) (MESERST, 2012) and consequently has the greatest number of yearly publications and yearly citations. The third rank of Université de Tunis Manar is explained by the fact that this University does not have a Center of Biotechnology that affords quality methods and materials as well as technical support for experimental research in biology and by the inactivity of certain of its specialized institutions like the Institute of Veterinary Research of Tunis established in 1897 (Wikimedia Foundation, 2015). This fact also explains the advantage of the Université de Sfax that have a center of biotechnology in the rankings that use Citations per paper rates to rank universities like Leiden. In fact, the rate of biological and medical scientists in the University of Sfax is the highest in Tunisia. So, it is the best university that issues important biological and Medical researches as shown in Fig. 2 and it is well known that such researches are receiving more citations that similar papers in other disciplines (Iglesias & Pecharromán, 2007). The standings of Université de Tunis Manar as second in such rankings are mainly explained by the excellence of this university in Medical Sciences and Pharmacology. This is mainly explained by the important impact of the works of Institut Pasteur de Tunis. In fact, this institution participates in international collaboration researches and these researches are known to be highly cited (Frame & Carpenter, 1979). This is also explained by the affiliation of many research hospitals and institutes within the Université de Tunis Manar allowing it to do quality medical trials and statistical researches unlike the universities of Sfax, Monastir and Sousse.

The Université de Tunis Manar as well as the Université de Sfax can enhance their standings in rankings like Leiden one by enhancing the interest of institutions not dealing with biological research like the Faculties of Economics and Management by doing interdisciplinary researches with leading biological research institutions. It is also advised that these two universities enhance research in their inactive biology research institutions like the National Institute of Veterinary Research in Tunis and the Institute of Olive trees in Sfax. This tendency to enhance Medical and Biological research in order to promote research standings of Tunisian Universities is not innovative as it is the perspective of the government for years (Naim & Rahman, 2008). But, more efforts should be done if Tunisian universities would like to be world class universities.

	Biological and Medical Sciences		Overall Standings	
Université de Manouba	0 Scholar	8	2 Scholar	7
Institut de Santé Publique	1 Scholar	6	1 Scholar	9
Université de Gabès	1 Scholar	6	2 Scholars	7
Université de Tunis	0 Scholar	8	4 Scholars	5
Université de Sousse	4 Scholars	5	4 Scholars	5
Université de Monastir	30 Scholars	3	34 Scholars	3
Université de Sfax	46 Scholars	1	51 Scholars	2
Université de Carthage	22 Scholars	4	31 Scholars	4
Université de Tunis Manar	40 Scholars	2	52 Scholars	1

Fig. 2: Repartitions of the Scientists and the Biological and Medical Scientists according to their affiliations

Other Rankings that do not classify the Universities of Tunis Manar and Sfax as first ones do not seem to be based on the research performances of universities excepting the one of the OIC that classify the University of Monastir as the first one. This is mainly explained by the fact that the University of Monastir was the university that published the most of papers between 2004 and 2006 (SESRTCIC, 2007). The other rankings like 4icu and Webometrics are mainly based on the presence of the universities in Internet including the existence of an official website, the existence of online resources and courses and the ads of the university or the average income of university professors and graduates (Al–Najjar, 2012). These factors seem to be economic and influenced by the expenses of the university in advertizing and engaging their students in job market and not related to the research performance of the Universities (Al–Najjar, 2012). It is important that even African countries with lower GDPs have better results than Tunisia in such rankings (Ndoye, 2010; Okorie, 2013). More interest should be given to such rankings even if they do not assess research quality of universities as they can harm the reputation of the country (Ndoye, 2010; Okorie, 2013). In fact, Higher education assessment is not just research assessment (Aguillo, Bar-Ilan, Levene, & Ortega, 2010).

It is also seen that some rankings have returned lower results for Tunisian Universities than expected like in THE. This is mainly due to the inaccuracy in entering affiliations by scientists in Tunisian Universities as they specify their institutions without citing their universities. In fact, we found institutions like ENIS apart from their universities in THE ranking.

Tunisian universities do not have any Social or Economic Scientist among the leading scientists of Tunisia. This is mainly explained for Social Sciences by a lack of citation indexing and behavior for the publications in Arabic and by that by the uncitedness of publications written in Arabic (Thomson Reuters, 2015). This is also explained for Social and Economic Sciences by the lack of originality in the choice of research topics in Tunisia.

2. Université de Carthage and Université de Monastir

As shown in Fig. 3, the Université de Carthage and the Université de Monastir are respectively the third and fourth universities of Tunisia. This is confirmed in rankings like SIR and is explained by the fact that these universities have the best number of professors and students after the ones of the Universities of Sfax and Tunis Manar (MESERST, 2012).

Field	Université de Carthage		Université de Monastir	
	Scientists	Rank	Scientists	Rank
Mathematics, Engineering and Computer Science	5	1	0	6
Medical Sciences and Pharmacology	0	6	28	2
Chemistry and Materials Science	1	3	1	3
Physics	3	1	3	1
Biology and Geological Sciences	22	2	2	4
Overall	31	4	34	3

Fig. 3: Dispersion of Scientists of Université de Carthage and Université de Monastir according to their disciplines

However, these Universities have succeeded to achieve the first and the second rank in several fields due to several factors:

The second rank of the Université de Monastir in Medical Sciences and Pharmacology is mainly explained by the affiliation of the unique Faculty of Pharmacy and the unique Faculty of Dental Medicine in Tunisia within the Université de Monastir (Wikimedia Foundation, 2015). But, it is clear when seeing the ranking of Tunisian scientists that most of the leading Tunisian Scientists of this field in the Université de Monastir do not work in Faculty of Dental Medicine of Monastir that seem to be inactive in research. More interest should be given to the promotion of Research in that institution.

The excellence of the Université de Carthage in Biological and Geological Sciences is mainly explained by the existence of the affiliation of the Center of Biotechnology of Borj Cedria as well as most of the leading institutions teaching Plant and Animal Science within the Université de Carthage. The results of the Université de Sfax are better thanks to their important interest to Bioinformatics and other interdisciplinary biological and geological disciplines unlike the Université de Carthage and it is known that interdisciplinary research has more citations than core research in biology (Iglesias & Pecharromán, 2007).

The excellence of the Université de Carthage in Physics and Mathematics, Engineering and Computer Science and its important results in Core Sciences like Chemistry and Materials Science is mainly explained by the affiliation of many nationwide leading institutions in these fields like INSAT, SupCom, IPEST and Polytechnic School of Tunisia within Université de Carthage.

The excellence of the Université de Monastir in Physics is mainly explained by the works of Ben Nasrallah et al. who are leading Thermodynamics Research in Tunisia and who have excellent Hirsch indexes (Turki & Turki, 2014). The inexistence of scientists in Physics other than Ben Nasrallah et al. and the poor performance of the Université de Monastir in other core sciences are mainly explained by the inactivity of several institutions like ISBM and the lack of availability of young researchers publishing quality works in these fields within the Université de Monastir. Some initiatives should be done to motivate such researchers to publish in important research journals.

3. Université de Tunis and Université de Sousse

As shown in Fig. 4, the Université de Tunis and the Université de Sousse are the fifth nationwide research universities as proved in many international rankings. This is mainly explained by the attribution of all the means and efficient laboratories of these universities to the Universities of Tunis Manar and Monastir when created (Wikimedia Foundation, 2015). Without such materials, the evolution of the parent universities is quite difficult explaining their current standings in this ranking as well as in many international research rankings and classifications.

Field	Université de Tunis		Université de Sousse	
	Scientists	Rank	Scientists	Rank
Mathematics, Engineering and Computer Science	3	3	0	6
Medical Sciences and Pharmacology	0	6	3	4
Physics	1	4	0	6
Biology and Geological Sciences	0	7	1	5
Overall	4	5	4	5

Fig. 4: Dispersion of Scientists of Université de Tunis and Université de Sousse according to their disciplines

The poor performance of the Université de Tunis is also explained by the inactivity of several institutions like ISG and TBS. These institutions are supposed to bring excellence of Université de Tunis in the Economic Sciences Research. The ENSIT has contributed to the better results of Mathematics, Engineering and Computer Science research. However, it did not contribute to efficiently enhance research in the core sciences like Chemistry and Materials Science and Physics within the Université de Tunis. More interest should be done to theadjustment of the research quality and interest in these faculties.

The poor performance of the Université de Sousse is also explained by the inactivity of several of its institutions. However, the most important reason of that is the deficiency of research in the Université de Sousse in Medical Sciences and Pharmacology that is still traditional and does not involve innovative and interdisciplinary techniques.

4. Other Universities of Tunisia

Generally, the other universities of Tunisia are universities with limited research productivity (Thomson Reuters, 2015) due to the limited number of professors in these universities (MESERST, 2012). As shown in Fig. 5, only the Universities of Gabes and Manouba and the Institut de Santé Publique have researchers within the Ranking of Tunisian Scientists issued in 2014.

Field	Université de Gabès		Institut de Santé Publique		Université de Manouba	
	Scientists	Rank	Scientists	Rank	Scientists	Rank
Mathematics, Engineering and Computer Science	0	6	0	6	2	4
Medical Sciences and Pharmacology	0	6	1	5	0	6
Chemistry and Materials Science	1	3	0	6	0	6
Biology and Geological Sciences	1	5	0	7	0	7
Overall	2	7	1	9	2	7

Fig. 5: Dispersion of Scientists of the other Universities of Tunisia according to their disciplines

The better results of the Université de Gabès and the Université de Manouba are mainly explained by the existence of quality specialized research institutions in Computer Science within the Université de Manouba and by the existence of FSG and ENIG that give interest to Chemistry Research and to the existence of theInstitute of Dry Regions of Medenine that gives interests to Biology research within the Université de Gabès (MESERST, 2012). Other public universities that have limited means and number of professors and that do not involve specialized research laboratories and institutions will be evidently inactive in research. The lack of interest, efficiency, proficiency and motivation of professors in research in these universities explains as well their limited research outputs. These universities do not unfortunately tend to ameliorate their reputation and situation in order to have international collaborations with several universities from European or North American universities or in order to have more citations even if they can easily do that. For example, Zitouna University was created in 737 and is the oldest university working nowadays (Wikimedia Foundation, 2015). However, it does not apply to the record in Guinness World Records book even if it can prove that it works since 737 with interruption and does not use this in order to do lobbying for the University and incite researchers to cite its researches and works.

Private Universities have poor standings in research in Tunisia just like in other Arab countries (Rugh, 2002). This is mainly explained by the lack of interest of these universities in research as it does not bring direct income to them (Rugh, 2002). These universities prefer to spend money in ads in order to incite students to enroll their courses as this will bring direct income to them instead of enrolling full professors and research to promote their research standings (Rugh, 2002). This fact is confirmed by the better standings of these universities in Webometrics and 4icu rankings and their inadequate standings in international research rankings.

Conclusion

Tunisian Universities can ameliorate their research performances if they can adjust the Research situation in their inactive institutions and if they can establish collaborations with other Universities and institutions in doing quality interdisciplinary research output. They can do that if they try to ameliorate their results in easily influenced factors of world rankings as cited in (Shahbazi-Moghadam, Salehi, Ale Ebrahim, Mohammadjafari, & Gholizadeh, 2015) and in (Docampo & Cram, 2014). For example, instead on working on increasing the number of citations and publications of universities, Tunisian universities can have better results using the same efforts if they try to increase their presence in the list of ISI highly cited scientists or in Science and Nature. In fact, this is how world class universities are bettering their standings in international rankings (Hoyler & Jons, 2008). In Tunisia, the University of Sousse tried to increase its standings in ARWU ranking by increasing the number of its ISI highly cited scientists. However, it failed to do that as the two scientists that are specialized in Mathematics, who were in the University of Sousse, and who are now in the list of 2015 ISI highly cited scientists have unfortunately left the University after 2012 to work in Saudi Arabia (Turki, 2015).

References

Aghion, P., Dewatripont, M., Hoxby, C., Sapir, A., & Mas-Colell, A. (2007). *Why reform Europe's universities?*

Aguillo, I. F., Ortega, J. L., & Fernández, M. (2008). Webometric ranking of world universities: Introduction, methodology, and future developments. *Higher education in Europe , 33* (2-3), 233-244.

Aguillo, I., Bar-Ilan, J., Levene, M., & Ortega, J. (2010). Comparing university rankings. *Scientometrics , 85* (1), 243-256.

Alaşehir, O. (2010). University Ranking by Academic Performance: A Scientometrics Study for Ranking World Universities. (Doctoral dissertation, Middle East Technical University).

Al-Najjar, S. (2012). University Rankings-New Method. *The international journal of social sciences , 5* (1), 37-44.

Cheng, Y., & Liu, N. C. (2007). Academic Ranking of World Universities by Broad Subject Fields 1. *Higher education in Europe , 32* (1), 17-29.

Docampo, D. (2010). On using the Shanghai ranking to assess the research performance of university systems. *Scientometrics , 86* (1), 77-92.

Docampo, D., & Cram, L. (2014). On the internal dynamics of the Shanghai ranking. *Scientometrics , 98* (2), 1347-1366.

Frame, J. D., & Carpenter, M. P. (1979). International research collaboration. *Social Studies of Science , 9* (4), 481-497.

Harfi, M., & Mathieu, C. (2006). Classement de Shanghai et image internationale des universités: quels enjeux pour la France? *Horizons stratégiques* (2), 100-115.

Hazelkorn, E. (2007). Les palmarès et les classements influencent-ils la prise de décision de l'enseignement supérieur. *Association Internationale des Universités, AIU Horizons , 13* (2-3), 4.

Hoyler, M., & Jons, H. (2008). Global knowledge nodes and networks.

Iglesias, J. E., & Pecharromán, C. (2007). Scaling the h-index for different scientific ISI fields. *Scientometrics , 73* (3), 303-320.

Ioannidis, J. P., Patsopoulos, N. A., Kavvoura, F. K., Tatsioni, A., Evangelou, E., Kouri, I., et al. (2007). International ranking systems for universities and institutions: a critical appraisal. *Bmc Medicine , 5* (1), 1.

Liu, N. C., Cheng, Y., & Liu, L. (2005). Academic ranking of world universities using scientometrics-A comment to the "Fatal Attraction". *Scientometrics , 64* (1), 101-109.

Mangematin, V., & Robin, S. (2003). The two faces of PhD students: Management of early careers of French PhDs in life sciences. *Science and Public Policy , 30* (6), 405-414.

MESERST. (2012). Statistiques de l"enseignement supérieur.

Naim, T. K., & Rahman, A. U. (2008). Mapping scientific research in OIC countries. Secretariat of the Standing Committee on Scientific and Technological Co-operation (COMSTECH) of the Organization of the Islamic Conference, Islamabad.

Ndoye, A. K. (2010). Réflexions sur un classement international des établissements universitaires africains. *Revue internationale d'éducation de Sèvres* (54), 117-125.

Okorie, P. (2013). Preliminary Assessment of National Universities Rankings as economic indicators in Africa. *European International Journal of Science and Technology* , 2 (8).

Rugh, W. A. (2002). Arab education: Tradition, growth and reform. *The Middle East Journal* , 396-414.

Salmi, J., & Saroyan, A. (2007). Les classements des universités comme instruments de politiques: usages constructifs pour l'enseignement supérieur. *Association Internationale des Universités, AIU Horizons* , 13 (2-3), 1-3.

SESRTCIC. (2007). *Academic Rankings of Universities in the OIC countries.* Retrieved from http://www.sesrtcic.org/files/article/232.pdf

Shahbazi-Moghadam, M., Salehi, H., Ale Ebrahim, N., Mohammadjafari, M., & Gholizadeh, H. (2015). Effective Factors for Increasing University Publication and Citation Rate. *Asian Social Science* , 11 (16), 338-348.

Thomson Reuters. (2015). *Journal Citation Report.*

Thomson Reuters. (2015). *Web of Science.*

Turki, H. (2015). Leading Tunisian scientists in Mathematics, Computer Science and Engineering. An Overview. GRIN Verlag.

Turki, H., & Turki, M. (2014). Ranking of Tunisian Scientists According to Their Efficient Productivity. An Overview of Scientific Research Output in Tunisia. Munich, Germany: GRIN Verlag.

Van Raan, A. F. (2005). Fatal attraction: Conceptual and methodological problems in the ranking of universities by bibliometric methods. *Scientometrics* , 62 (1), 133-143.

Wagner, C. S., & Leydesdorff, L. (2005). Network structure, self-organization, and the growth of international collaboration in science. *Research policy* , 34 (10), 1608-1618.

Wikimedia Foundation. (2015). Wikipedia, the free encyclopedia.

YOUR KNOWLEDGE HAS VALUE

- We will publish your bachelor's and
  master's thesis, essays and papers

- Your own eBook and book -
  sold worldwide in all relevant shops

- Earn money with each sale

Upload your text at www.GRIN.com
and publish for free